T0130107

Fierce & Fabulous

A Young Lady's Guide To Inspiration And Positive Self-Image

Glynis Whitted Bell

authorHOUSE®

AuthorHouse™
1663 Liberty Drive
Bloomington, IN 47403
www.authorhouse.com
Phone: 1 (800) 839-8640

Published by AuthorHouse 02/10/2016

ISBN: 978-1-5049-7473-8 (sc)
ISBN: 978-1-5049-7472-1 (e)

Library of Congress Control Number: 2016900993

Print information available on the last page.

Any people depicted in stock imagery provided by Thinkstock are models,
and such images are being used for illustrative purposes only.
Certain stock imagery © Thinkstock.

This book is printed on acid-free paper.

Glynis Whitted Bell, Author

Girls of all kinds can be beautiful--from the thin, plus sized, short, very tall, ebony to porcelain-skinned; the quirky, clumsy, shy, outgoing and all in between. It's not easy though because many people still put beauty into a confining narrow box…Think outside the box…Pledge that you will look in the mirror and find the unique beauty in you.
Tyra Banks--Former supermodel, television personality, talk show host, actress and author.

A YOUNG LADY'S GUIDE TO INSPIRATION AND POSITIVE SELF-IMAGE

Dedication

To my precious daughter, my mini me, Isley; to my mother Mary Whitted; my grandmothers, Ethel N. Whitted and Bernice Liggins, who were beautiful and strong role models for me. Not only did they train, teach, nurture, and discipline me into the woman that I am today, but they also led by example. To all of my aunties, Godmother, church mothers, teachers, who have also played a huge role in being a part of my village, I am grateful. A huge thanks to Trice Hickman, an author, undergraduate colleague and friend, who read my very raw manuscript and said, "I believe in what you are doing Glynis; I know that you can do this." And to my Uncle Richard Whitted, I know that you are looking down from Heaven, and I hope that you are proud of me!

Author's Note

First impressions REALLY are everything and IMAGE really does matter. Image is more than just clothes; it's hair, it's a look, it's confidence, it's all about a total package, which totals a confident, young lady! Long gone are the days where mom and grandma were the two most influential figures in a young girl's life. Today the media, social media, YouTube and popular apps are "helping" to shape, mold, and dress our girls. This book is designed to inspire and share some simple ways to help young girls put their best foot forward whether it's a school day, place of worship event, internship, hanging out with friends or a date.

WOW what a journey! I had never seriously considered writing a book. Nevertheless, in March 2011, I called upon a dynamic group of phenomenal female friends to celebrate Women's History Month as a fundraiser for Dress for Success Winston-Salem, a non-profit organization that I founded in 2009. The theme of the event was "Her Inspiration to Write." Several authors shared their own stories of why they write and what it means to express themselves through the written word. After that event, the spark to share my passion with young women was born, and I started writing my thoughts on a legal pad. I kept that pad beside my bed and from time to time throughout the rest of the year, I wrote a little bit here and there. Out of fear, I didn't tell anyone that I was writing a book; fear of what people would say or think or even if what I had written was worthy of sharing with anyone. It wasn't until January 2012 that I committed to transferring my work to the computer. It then became a reality. I started envisioning my platform, how the book would look, and what kind of pen I would use for book-signing events.

In May 2012, I was asked to speak to the Girls Take the Lead group at Philo Middle School in Winston-Salem under the direction of Julie Puckett. That meeting was a true turning point in my writing journey. I told the group that I was writing a book and wanted to share with them some of the concepts in the book. That was the first time I had publically shared any of my work with the audience for which it was intended. I held my breath as I asked each of the seven girls to pick a letter of the alphabet so that I could share my heartfelt thoughts with them. I breathed a sigh of relief when my thoughts were well received and their feedback was positive. That was the validation that I needed to keep writing.

Another crucial point in my journey was attending a workshop called WRITE Now! in June 2012. This workshop organized by Alicia Clinton, author of *Destined for Success*, was not only inspirational but motivational. The workshop helped me see my vision more clearly and offered me the opportunity to design a book cover so that I could have a constant visual reminder of what my finished product would look like.

I put lots of thought and consideration into the creation and purpose of this book. The capital letters are created to be inspirational, uplifting, and motivational. The lower case letters are designed to share a tip, drop some knowledge and school young girls on fashion and how to look their best whatever they do and wherever they go.

I would like to give heartfelt thanks to my some very special people who supported me through this process. My husband and children, for knowing that Sunday evenings were my writing time and they honored that. My parents for their undying support and love. My sister for believing in me and having my back. To Deb and Anita for their review and feedback and for being the best of friends and roommates! To Karen Russell and Nakida McDaniels for their review and feeback. To my (long distance) editor Dr. Dwedor Morais Ford, for her endless hours of Sunday evening phone calls, encouragement, understanding my many trains of thought, for her patience and commitment. And to my (local) editor, John X. Miller for his attention to detail, insistence of paragraph and coma additions and making sure that the manuscript was word perfect. And to the countless others who supported, encouraged, uplifted and believed in me and this project. You all are so important to me!

A-a

Always have an honest friend in your circle and a full-length mirror in your home

Whenever I see people out and they look a hot mess, I conclude that they are missing two important things in their lives: an honest friend and a full-length mirror. An honest friend will tell you if you look a hot mess with love or say, "You CANNOT go out with me wearing that!" Take a look at yourself in a full-length mirror, from head to toe...what do you see? Seeing is believing—Believe in YOU! If in doubt when you pass by your full-length mirror on your way out of the house, ask yourself would I hire me? Would I date me? Would I be seen with me? If the answer is yes, then you are moving in the right direction; but if the answer is no, then read on!

accessories are a girl's best friend

Accessories are a girl's best friend, friends are a girl's best accessory; accessories always look good, fit just right, don't care if you're not the right shade, and never go out of style! This is an original saying from a postcard I created several years ago. Being an accessory lover, I like to think of accessories as the icing on the cake. If you have ever eaten a piece of birthday cake that was piled high with frosting, you may have forgotten that there was cake underneath. This is the same way you can look at accessories with an outfit; if you wear too many, then whatever is underneath will surely be lost. Accessories should be added to complete a look.

While we're still on A, let's talk about one of my favorite A words: Appropriate.

appropriate: to set apart for a particular use or purpose

Whatever the occasion, young ladies should be appropriately dressed. I once attended two separate school events. As a keen observer of people, I was amazed at how inappropriately some of the students were dressed. The students were asked to wear dark bottoms and solid colored shirts.

What I saw was far from what was expected because the rules left too much room for self-interpretation. The students wore floral skirts, and sequined shirts, party dresses and the list goes on. Let me say for the record that people have the right to express themselves by the choice of their attire; however, there are times, such as during public events like school band concerts, where the goal is not to be distracted by what the performers are wearing but to hear a beautiful performance. Perhaps the rules should have been more specific; for example students should have been told to wear black pants or skirts and white-collar shirts. Most people already have those items already in their closets. This "uniform" would have solved the problem of appropriateness and helped with uniformity.

In this case, school uniforms help with being appropriate and keep distractions about what students are wearing to a minimum. They also promote school pride. When I was in graduate school, I wrote a research paper on school uniforms. I was on the fence (and still am to a certain extent) on whether school uniforms do what they are designed to do. I see pros and cons to the school uniform argument.

Both my children have attended public schools that required school uniforms. Starting in elementary school, they were required to wear a uniform. In middle school they didn't have a dress code and in high school they have what's called SMOD (standard mode of dress.) I can attest firsthand to the benefits and challenges that wearing school uniforms can bring. My son didn't seem to mind having to wear a uniform to school. I think for him, wearing a uniform takes the guesswork out of getting dressed in the morning. However, my daughter's thoughts on attending a high school that has dress restrictions is a sore subject all together. My kids aren't the only ones with their own thoughts on schools mandating dress codes.

What I gathered from an August 2012 newspaper article from the *Winston Salem Chronicle* was that students, parents, and principals' thoughts on school uniforms are most often an interesting contrast. In the article, several students were interviewed about their thoughts on having SMOD at a local high school for the first time. One student stated, "It will help me because when you go for interviews and go to work places, you have to dress up anyway so this will help me get used to it." Another student said she didn't like the dress code one bit and felt that students should have their own say about what they can wear, since they are adults now. The student also said that the restrictive dress code was cramping her personal style and that it took away from her individuality. The principal said that the first day of school under the new dress code policy went well. He also said, "Kids don't want to admit it, but they are conducting themselves very appropriately."

According to a news report, a Florida school board member suggested to the school board that a dress code should be established for the parents while they attend meetings or school events. It had been noted that parents would show up in less than appropriate attire, often wearing pajama bottoms, house slippers and skin revealing shorts and shirts to school. The suggestion didn't pass the school board vote. However, it did create lots of conversation about the need to even think of having a dress code for parents.

There will always be a need for uniform dress in certain work, such as in sports, and military situations. The overall goal of a uniform is to create well… uniformity. This doesn't mean that uniformity has to take away from your talents and your personality. You should be able to shine no matter what you're wearing. Most of how you look at life goes back to your ATTITUDE, another one of my favorite A words! A positive attitude can trump a bad outfit any day! However, I can't stress enough to dress appropriately for whatever the occasion.

Every girl should own a solid black skirt (not too short) and a well-fitting pair of black slacks (not too tight) and a white-collar shirt (that won't gap open when buttoned); if you don't have these items, invest in them now! These three wardrobe staples can be worn for many occasions, and I can almost bet that this combination can help create an ensemble that will be appropriate for many occasions!

Lillian D. Bjorseth, a networking expert, once said, "Dress for the occasion. If the occasion is business, then dress like you mean business." Later in the book, I will talk about the definitions for appropriate dress; for example, Business Casual and After 5 Attire.

attract what you project

Oftentimes young ladies attract what they project; in other words, the message that they send out based on what they wear, how they act, and how they carry themselves, draws a certain kind of attention. It's no wonder they are being hit on and asked out by scrubs. Have you heard "Scrubs" by the group TLC, a popular hit song from the 1990's? Check it out on YouTube, then you can decide if you are dressing or acting like a scrub magnet! Bottom line... young ladies respect yourselves and set high standards WITHOUT compromise!

Mirror, Mirror -- When was the last time you noticed someone you thought was dressed inappropriately and why? What was the occasion? What would you have changed to make the outfit appropriate? How do you feel about wearing a uniform for school or work?

ℬ-b

"Beauty isn't worth thinking about; what's important
is your mind. You don't want a fifty-dollar haircut on a
fifty-cent head." Garrison Keillor -- American author,
storyteller, humorist, and radio personality.

Be your own kind of beautiful!

Raising a daughter is no easy task. Between competing with technology and society to raise a self-confident and well-rounded young lady to providing the basic daily necessities, raising a daughter can be daunting to say the least.

Both of my children were born prematurely. My daughter was born three months prematurely and weighed in at a whopping 1 pound, 5.8 ounces. Needless to say, life has been an amazing roller coaster ride since they both came into the world.

One of the traits that I recognized early on with my daughter, even with her severe prematurity, was the fact that she was very independent and opinionated. (Yes, we bump heads about that sometimes.) When she was 15 years old, I began to see her blossoming and developing into a strong and colorful young woman.

I recall a trip that she and I made to the MAC makeup counter. We were enjoying playing in the candy store of colors. For the record—I love makeup! She often asks when she can start wearing makeup. I say when you're older and before she can get the next statement out of her mouth, I say, "and I don't care that some of your friends are wearing it now!" But, when we get to the counter, I let her sit in the chair to get a little lip gloss. On this day, the male makeup artist engaged her by answering her makeup questions (never a shortage of questions with her ever; a good trait she is developing.) She asked the makeup artist if he could make a mole on the left side of her face go away. He responded, "That's a beauty mark honey and women pay lots of money to get those—it makes you unique; you'll appreciate it more when you're older." Ever since that day, she has not asked about making the mole disappear; but she is learning daily to be her own kind of beautiful!

be a keeper to a brotha and if applicable, encourage him to pull up his pants. That's a whole 'nother book all together. But ladies, don't sell yourselves short, if you look your best, you can help our brothas do better. Sagging is NOT a good look!

C-c

Create the person you want to become, starting NOW.

It's never too early for young ladies to start dressing for and acting like where they're going; great places no doubt! It amazes me to see young people dressed to impress; they stand out. It is so easy nowadays to follow the crowd; but if a young lady takes that extra step to go above and beyond, it will pay off and she will get noticed…for the right reasons! It saddens me to see young people presenting themselves in less than positive ways: sagging, wearing outfits that are too tight and too revealing, swearing loudly, disrespecting themselves and those around them, mean mugging, having bad attitudes, and the list goes on.

Never underestimate the value of a simple smile. Kirk Franklin's song, "I Smile" is one of those songs that no matter where I am, no matter what kind of day I may be having, when I hear it, well, I smile! (and sing along, of course). Some of my favorite lines of the song go like this: "You look so much better when you smile, so smile"; "I know God is working so I smile"; and "Today's a new day, but there is no sunshine." This last line reminds me of a story. One overcast day, I was heading to lunch wearing a bright yellow and white shirt. I ran into someone who stopped me on the sidewalk and said, "I like your shirt, it's all bright and cheery." I replied, "And on a day like today, we need a little sunshine in our lives, especially when the weather is gray." Then she said, "I guess sometimes you have to bring your own sunshine." I smiled and thought some days, you have to bring your own sunshine and shine wherever you are.

Smiling is infectious and will definitely make a difference in you and no doubt in those people with whom you come in contact. Sometimes the best looking thing anyone can wear is a smile and a pleasant attitude. Both are more fashionable than any name brand on the market. And even though I can't wear that shirt every day, when I do, I am reminded to bring my own sunshine!

> "Wherever you go, no matter what the weather always bring your own sunshine"-Anthony J D'Angelo -- Author and Founder of Collegiate EmPowerment.

clothes don't make the wo(man).

Wear the clothes; don't let them wear you. Have you ever noticed people, but really didn't see them because you couldn't get past what they were wearing? Many people spend lots of time and money searching for the "perfect" outfit for special occasions such as weddings (especially if you are not the bride), concerts, parties, proms, family reunions, and class reunions (especially when you get older).

I have a thought about that; many times, when shopping under pressure, we select the wrong items, spend too much money, dislike the items we purchase, which usually hang in the back of the closet and never get worn again. I recently learned of a new trend in subscription-type shopping that may be the answer to this what-am-I-going-to wear special occasion- dressing dilemma. Think Netflix for fashion. There are a couple of options such as The Fashion Library and Rent the Runway. These subscription-based services allow you to pick that fancy dress, killer shoes and to-die-for necklace and purse to wear for that special occasion and for a reasonable price, wear them, look fabulous and then return them without having to buy them for keeps! Pretty cool concept, huh? Even more reason to keep in mind, that more than likely, the other people attending the event who may have been in that same what-am-I going-to-wear dilemma, won't remember what you wore; but they will remember if you looked healthy and if you were enjoying yourself. And you can't enjoy yourself if you are not comfortable!

"A woman's dress should be like a barbed-wire fence:
serving its purpose without obstructing the view."--
Sophia Loren, popular actress in the 1960's. First
female celebrity to launch her own fragrance line.

compliments-They are okay to give and to receive, sincerely

There is nothing wrong with admiring other people's styles; there is also nothing wrong with giving a sincere compliment and being able to receive one. The easiest way to receive a compliment is to simply and graciously say, "Thank you." Complimenting people is a nice thing to do and most likely will catch them off guard but will usually bring a smile to their face; and chances are, the compliment will make their day. Compliments can also open the door to a new friendship or acquaintance. Try giving someone a sincere compliment today.

Mirror, Mirror -- When was the last time you received a compliment? What were you complimented on? How did it make you feel? When was the last time you complimented someone else and what did you compliment them on?

Couldn't-Shouldn't-Wouldn't-wear that!

One Monday morning, I was walking behind a young lady who worked in the same building with me. Her make-up and hair were nicely done. She had on a great pair of wedges and had a perfect pair of legs. BUT, the dress she had on left little to the imagination; it was way too short and jacked up in the back! As I walked behind her, I couldn't help but wonder, what she would do if she dropped something and had to bend over to pick it up; did she think to look at herself in a full-length mirror? (Revisit letter A) I was embarrassed for her, as her look was so close to being complete, but the one flaw, the dress being too short and a little too casual, ruined the entire look. Lesson: Use the mirror, get a second opinion from a trusted friend, and if in doubt, make a change!

Once while I was working in a corporate environment as a contractor, I was offered a full-time position at the company. In an effort to bring someone else up the corporate ladder, just as someone had helped me get to the next level, I recommended a young college graduate to fill my contracting position. This young aspiring designer was a true fashionista. She had her own unique style that pushed the limits of what was sometimes acceptable for corporate America. One day after meeting with a group of managers, there was a buzz about what the young associate was wearing. As I recall, it was an ensemble that included red and white vertically striped tights. I overheard one of the managers say, "She looks like the witch in the *Wizard of Oz* that the house fell on." I realized at that point, she had lots of potential in the industry and it would be a shame to have her career cut short because of her choice of attire.

I went to her supervisor, who was also a friend of mine, and shared with her the manager's comments. I recommended that the manager speak with the young woman about toning down her choice of outfits. This must have worked as the young contractor went on to become a designer and had great success working for the company and beyond. The point was not to change her style but to adjust it to her environment so that her wardrobe would not be career prohibitive.

Mirror Mirror -- How do you handle "constructive criticism"? Constructive criticism is the process of offering valid and well-reasoned opinions about the work of others, usually involving both positive and negative comments, in a friendly manner rather than an oppositional one. The purpose of constructive criticism is to improve the outcome.

D-d

Don't *look like your situation*

I remember hearing a message my minister, Bishop Sir Walter Mack, Jr. gave about not looking like your situation. I thought about what he said and came up with this; if you are broke down and going through a rough time, you don't have to look like it! Put on your favorite ensemble, a smile, and make up your mind not to look like you may feel. This is not always an easy thing to do. Sometimes in life when you are going through a rough time, and want to be left alone at your own pity party in your favorite T-shirt and sweats, and you can cry if you want to. (FACTOID-According to Wikipedia, "It's My Party" was a No.1 hit on the Pop and R&B Charts in 1965, sung by Lesley Gore and was the first hit single for mega producer Quincy Jones. The song lyrically portrays the unhappiness of a teenage girl at her birthday party when her boyfriend Johnny disappears, only to hook up with Judy who is "wearing his ring," to indicate she's replaced the birthday girl as his love interest.)

The song's chorus, "It's my party, and I'll cry if I want to... You would cry too if it happened to you!" became a part of American pop culture language as a phrase used to describe being utterly humiliated and miserable during an event that is supposed to be a happy occasion.

We all experience those ups and downs in life. I often say that "life is what happens after the best plans are made." You may fail a test (even after studying), you may lose a friend or a loved one, and the one you thought was Mr. Right may turn out to be Mr. WRONG! BUT you don't have to let life's low points bring you down and keep you there. Cry, wipe those tears, and keep the party going in a positive direction!

A soon-to-be-90-year-young woman was asked to share 40 lessons that life had taught her. On her list of 40 was, "No matter how you feel, get up, dress up and show up!" I hope that if I make it to 90, or even close, I'll be thinking that same thing.

ditch *anything too tight, too low, too revealing…you get the point!*

Ladies, if you are going to take the time and effort to buy an article of clothing, make sure you buy it to FIT! The size printed on the label inside does not matter; what matters is how it fits your body and that it fits properly. When you raise your arms, others don't need to see your stomach. When you bend over, others don't need to see your backside. When you lean forward, we don't need to see your tatas. All designers sizing are not the same; for example, a size 10 in one designer's outfit, could mean a size 8 or 12 in another's. In my closet, I have every size from small to extra-large and 6 to 16. Don't worry about "the number" in the garment; be sure you are comfortable with the way it looks and fits your body! I would love to create a line of clothing called "Fitums." Whatever you put on would fit perfectly. The line would be all about the fit and the comfort of the garments and NOT the size on the tag. If my career as an author doesn't work out, then perhaps I will become a designer!

> "Dear girls, dressing immodestly is like rolling around in manure. Yes, you'll get attention, but mostly from pigs"--
> Sincerely, real men. (Someecards.com)

I was once at the mall and discovered something pretty cool. It's called Me-ality™, a scanning device that takes your exact measurements and translates them into your size in different store brands. Me-ality™ is a free service that takes less than ten minutes to process. With the help of a lovely assistant, I stepped into a machine that looked like something out of the latest sci fi thriller. It didn't swallow me up and spit me out; but it did do a full body scan to capture my true measurements. The information from the scan is put into a computer, which prints out a list to be used at the stores in the mall.

What was also super cool is that if you purchased an item from the list and brought your receipt back to the scanning kiosk, you would get a $ 5 gift card to use elsewhere at the mall. So, as I am discovering, there are services that can help determine what size you wear. These services are free, painless, and could save you a lot of time and headaches during your shopping adventures. Jeans and swimsuits are two of the hardest items to find the correct fit; this is where Me-ality™ can make shopping for those items a breeze! Check out Me-ality.com

E-e

Exercise your right to fashion freedom (within limits)

You don't have to be a fashion clone. And you don't have to be the one who stands out in the crowd…for the wrong reasons! It is true that we come in all different shapes and sizes. The beautiful thing is that our master pattern maker knew what he was doing when he created us. Thank goodness, he didn't create us all alike; what a boring place this would be! While you're exercising your right to fashion freedom, EXERCISE your body. No matter what shape you are in, it's never too late to make sure that you take care of your body and look and feel your personal best. A little activity each day can make a big difference. Whatever physical activities you enjoy doing, make it a part of your daily routine. Put down the remote control and walk around the block, plug in your earbuds and dance, go to the park and swing; whatever you enjoy doing, do it because nothing that you can put ON your body can ever replace taking care of your body.

"Be yourself: everyone else is taken." – Oscar
Wilde, Irish playwright and poet.

exceptions to every rule

I can imagine that both Lady Gaga's and Nicki Minaj's moms were glad when they made it big in the entertainment industry and were able to make money for their choices in fashion and entertainment "creativity." There will always be individuals who catch the limelight for extreme measures. This can be a negative as well as a positive. Think Miley Cyrus and Beyonce: they have certainly had their share of TMZ moments. Ranging from run-ins with the law, on stage fashion fails, and sometimes ratchett behavior on and off the stage. Often times, celebrities look at any publicity as "good" publicity. Back in my day, my two favorite artists who did this exceptionally well were Prince and Madonna. They created their own public relations buzz by their interesting choice of dress and their "creative" stage performances.

Willow Smith is another example of what I would call an entertainment rebel. And rebel, not necessarily in a negative way. Willow Smith's song "Whip my Hair" rocked the pop charts in 2010 and had even me whipping my hair back and forth (HEADACHE!) as I danced along to the catchy lyrics.

She too is known for her "eclectic" style. According to the Merriam Webster dictionary online, eclectic (☐☐kl☐kt☐k) is an adjective when used in art and philosophy and means "selecting what seems best from various styles, doctrines, ideas, methods, etc." The second definition of eclectic fits Willow to a tee. It is "composed of elements drawn from a variety of sources, styles, etc." Whenever you see her, you never know what fashion trends and hairstyles she may be rocking. Willow is a product of an entertainment family and growing up with these influences may allow her to get away with the weird and wonderful. However, the industry can often dictate what rules we can make and break when it comes to how we look, what's accepted and what is frowned upon.

(*Little-known fact*: According to Wikipedia Jada Pinkett Smith, mom of Willow Smith, attended The North Carolina School of the Arts in Winston-Salem, North Carolina in 1989.)

"I don't consider my own clothing to be outrageous...the truth is the people just don't have the same references that I do. To me, it's very beautiful and it's art and to them it's outrageous and crazy."-- Lady GaGa, American singer, songwriter and actress.

embrace you!

One day I was in Walmart strolling the aisles and people watching. Well, what I didn't know at the time was someone was people watching me. Put a pin here, you never know who may be checking you out! A lady approached me and asked me what I used to make my hair curly. I smiled and started sharing with her my many product trials and errors. She had a product in her hand and said that she had tried lots of different hair products to get the perfect curls, but nothing was working. A few minutes into the conversation, I said to her, "Your curls are beautiful just like they are; embrace YOU." She looked at me and said, "You are right, I need to embrace me." I thought about that interaction as I was walking to my car and this came to mind; no amount of product in a jar, bottle, or tube can make you look or feel better until you have embraced YOU!

education is the key to unlock doors to success

I enjoyed my high school and undergraduate college years immensely and was very active in activities in high school and college. I was the SGA president my senior year in high school and my classmates voted me as most dependable. I was the President of my junior class in college, runner up to Miss Winston-Salem State University and sang in the University Choir my freshman year. I have often said that I would love to go back and re-do my senior year in college knowing what I know now and wonder what I may have done differently.

When I graduated from Winston-Salem State University in Winston-Salem, North Carolina many years ago, I gave a brief thought to becoming a flight attendant. I thought it would be fun to jet set all over the world, meeting wonderful people and shopping! I never did pursue that as a career choice but went on to do other things academically and professionally. I had never seriously considered returning to school after I completed my undergraduate degree until I began to look into what I wanted to *be* when I grew up. I looked at what I loved to do and asked myself, "Self, what would you love to do every day that you would do even if you weren't getting paid to do it?" And (my)self immediately responded... "SHOPPING!"

I realized that I had always had a passion for fashion and would love to pursue something in that field. I researched the Textile, Design and Marketing program at the University of North Carolina at Greensboro (UNCG.) Other than working in retail part-time, I didn't have any experience in that area. But I did have the passion! I thought that if I could put some education behind my passion, I would be unstoppable!

I started the graduate program at UNCG in the fall of 2002. At the time, I had just gotten a contract position working at Sara Lee (now Hanesbrands.) So I returned to graduate school part-time and started a new job in the field of textiles. I was hoping that my new schooling and my new career would be a match made in heaven. It wasn't heaven initially, because perfect matches often take time to create, but I learned to enjoy the journey and learned valuable lessons along the way. Prior to creating a career track, I was working in J.O.B.S (**J**ourney **O**f the **B**roke). It was difficult returning to school as an adult with a family and working full time, but I was determined to make it work. It consisted of long nights, sacrificing weekend activities, and not to mention the exams and the research papers. But anything worth having is worth working hard for!

My son is a currently a college freshman. We were both excited and nervous about the process of applying to schools. The application process alone can be overwhelming! I know that things have changed alot since I applied to college. I'm not only referring to the application process, but the resources that students have access to and the accommodations and amenities that are available to them once they set foot on campus. Long gone are the days of pay phones on the dorm halls, cafeteria-only dining and non air-conditioned dorm rooms. I was recently on a tour of High Point University in High Point, North Carolina. After the tour, I immediately wanted to become an undergraduate student again. The campus is beautiful! They have snack stations for students, an outdoor pool, a game room and a movie theatre ON CAMPUS! WOW, how cool is that?

The students appeared to be happy and excited about learning in this type of environment. What better combination than to match fun and education in the same place. I encourage my son and all students thinking about next steps on their educational journey to enjoy it, don't wish to grow up too fast and value the learning process. Learning is lifelong and investing in yourself will **always** yield positive results!

"Education is our passport to the future, for tomorrow belongs to the people who prepare for it today"--Malcolm X, American Muslim Minister and human rights activist.

Mirror, Mirror -- What are some of your educational goals? If you don't think that college is the path that you want to take, then what are some other options that you could consider?

𝓕-𝓯

First impressions really are everything

They say don't judge a book by its cover, and that you only get one chance to make a first impression. (Did you judge my book by its cover?) Can you recall a time when you met someone who made a lasting impression on you? Was it what they wore? Was it their confidence? Was it what they said or how they carried themselves? If you remember them for one of these reasons, then it must have worked. What will you be remembered for?

In 1990 the popular movie "Pretty Woman", made its debut on the big screen. actor Richard Gere played the character of Edward, a wealthy businessman, and actress Julia Roberts played the role of Vivian, a prostitute. Edward hired Vivian to be his date to several social functions over the course of a week. This romantic comedy unfolded with Edward needing to change Vivian's look so that she would not look like what she was. Before her transformation, she went into a fancy store to look around. She was wearing a short skirt, knee high boots, and smacking on a wad of gum. She looked like she couldn't afford to shop there. The store clerk ignored her and turned up her nose (threw shade) at Vivian in disgust. After her transformation into a lady, she went back into the store, this time wearing a nice dress, with her hair done, and she looked like she could afford to shop there. She walked into the store carrying shopping bags, evidence of her shopping at other stores that day. The store clerk immediately greeted her and asked her if she could help her with anything. Vivian smiled and asked the clerk if she worked on commission. When she replied, "Yes," Vivian flaunted her packages and walked out of the store. This time it was Vivian who was smiling with satisfaction.

The moral of this story is that Vivian was the same person as the first time she came into the store looking like a prostitute, as she was when she returned looking as if she could afford it all. This was one of the more memorable parts of the movie. Here are the points that I'm making:

- Perception of who you are may not come close to the real thing; so don't give someone a reason to doubt you before can prove otherwise.
- If you present yourself in an appropriate and positive manner, you will more than likely be treated in a manner that will produce positive results.
- Play your role and train your audience to respect your acting skills. Life is not a dress rehearsal, so get it right the first time the curtain opens. You never know when the spotlight will be shining on you.
- You don't have to look like your situation.
- Sometimes you may have to fake it (give it the Oscar-winning effort) 'til you make it!

I was recently thrift shopping at one of my fav thrift boutiques when I saw a group of people gathering for what appeared to be a meeting or training. One young woman stood out in the crowd to me; she was wearing shorts, a T-shirt, and a sleep bonnet on her head. (I want to state for the record . . . I don't think that it is EVER acceptable to wear pajama bottoms and a satin bonnet outside of your home!) I was a little confused, thinking hummm . . . I hope she didn't show up for the meeting looking like that? Well curiosity got the best of me, and I asked one of the employees why the crowd was there. He said they were there for community service orientation. A number of thoughts went through my mind:

1. No matter what the reason, dress your personal best because you never know who you may encounter along the way.
2. I wanted to pull her inside the dressing room and do an ambush makeover.
3. Perhaps she didn't have a good friend or mentor to say, "You may NOT want to wear that to your meeting."

foundational garments are essential to complete the overall look

It all starts with the foundation; a house built on a solid and smooth foundation is the kind of house we all want. So setting the foundation for what you put on the outside of your body is essential to how it will look and perform. Having the proper undergarments are equally, if not, more important than the clothes. Most women don't know what size bra they wear. Get professionally measured. This is also very applicable when you have lost or gained weight! (Most bra retailers will measure you at no cost.) Just as you have a wardrobe of various jeans and tops to wear for certain occasions, it is important to invest in a foundational garment wardrobe to choose from based on your choice of attire.

Bra strap mishaps and snap backs-my how things have changed. There was a time when showing of one's undergarments was a no-no in public and if they were seen the person was either an entertainer or a lady of the night. Today however, it seems that PSU (public show of underwear) is no longer a secret, not Victoria's anyway! Slips and pantyhose are almost unheard of and definitely not used. But bra straps and thongs are on display like art in a museum. I don't wish to see thongs displayed through clinging knit maxi dresses or peeking over the tops of low cut jeans when you bend over. There's a bra with cups, but no straps, that is specifically made to be worn with spaghetti-strap dresses and tanks tops so that you would have the support and coverage you need.

Also created for discretion is the "wear it 12 ways kinda bra" or a bandeau/tube top. There are also no show panty line panties designed to be invisible under certain fabrics. There are solutions to fix the mishaps. It's identifying what they are and being willing to change them that makes the difference. Snap backs? Really...we called those baseball caps.

"God made a very obvious choice when he made me voluptuous; why would I go against what he decided for me? My limbs work, so I'm not going to complain about the way my body is shaped." --Drew Barrymore, famous child star, model, producer, director and author.

G-g

Get motivated!

Give back to your community. Get moving! Go Green! Good posture=good presence! Repeat after me; Good, Better, Best, I will not rest, until my good become better and my better becomes best! Consider volunteering with an organization that you are interested in. Volunteering is an opportunity to meet new people, give back to your community and learn more about the work that others do to enhance the quality of life in the neighborhoods where you live.

When I was in college, I did two internships. Both of which gave me the opportunity to work in a field that I was interested in; broadcast journalism. It allowed me the opportunity to network with professionals in the industry and to add value and experience to my growing resume. It gave me experience that I could use for internship credit as well as business contacts that I still keep in contact with today. Most students are required to do a certain number of community service hours for class or organizational credit; make it count by doing something you enjoy and making valuable contacts for future opportunities. Work smarter, not harder!

good grooming is essential

Basic grooming includes cleansing, manicuring, pedicuring, trimming, brushing, and styling just to name a few. Yes, these things can be done professionally, but do-at-home grooming is easy, inexpensive, and NOT optional. I believe in the life- changing properties of soap and water. If you don't believe me, you can ask any of my college roommates or my family. They tease me about my bathing frequency and water usage! I think a part of grooming includes smelling nice. I like to smell good and wear scents according to my mood; sassy some days, other days sweet! Nowadays, there is no shortage of celebrity fragrance creations and after sampling a few, perhaps celebrities should stick to entertaining not fragrance making! My point is, too much of a good thing can be bad. I shouldn't be able to smell you before I see you and after you leave. At a place that I worked, when a salesman came into our office, there was no mistaking he was there or had been there because you could smell his cologne. It was probably a very expensive brand, but each time he came in, it smelled as if he had used the entire bottle.

Fragrance is a very personal thing. Just because we love a particular scent doesn't mean we need to force others to like it, too. Oftentimes, we become immune to it if we wear it all the time. One perfume on a friend could smell divine and on another it could smell like muddy swine -- aka pigs. I have said it before: all things in moderation, no exception with wearing fragrances. Just a little bit will do the trick; consider this especially if you are going to be in close quarters with other people. Many people have allergies and a strong fragrance worn in close spaces could be the trigger to set off sneezes, coughs and watery eyes.

$\mathcal{H}\text{-}h$

Haters should be your elevators and motivators

According to the online Urban Dictionary a hater is "A person who develops a strong dislike for another, solely based on their opinion or personal judgment rather than objective merit." A hater's contempt commonly arises from jealousy and/or resentment. Additionally, the word "hater" is frequently overused mainly in the rap and hip-hop community. In life, you will have people who don't like you because of what you wear or how you talk, where you live or for reasons for which you may not be aware.

"There will be haters, there will be doubters, there will be non-believers, and then there will be YOU, proving THEM wrong."-- Karina Barton, Clinical Hypnotherapist.

have a go-to, make-you-feel-like-a-million dollars, take-on-the-world, kick-butt-kinda ensemble.

Have an outfit that on your worst day you can put on and feel like you can conquer the world! Once upon a time, I had just such an outfit. It consisted of a black blazer, great fitting pair of black slacks, a green blouse (my fav. color), a bold multicolored silk scarf and a pair of black loafers. It's been years since I owned this ensemble, but I remember it as my go-to, conquer-the-world, don't-fret-over-the-fashion outfit. Whenever I wore this outfit, I got compliments. I always felt confident and in control when I wore it. We all need an outfit that we feel like a million dollars in. Create one and take a selfie or two in it and use it as a reminder when you need a little pick me up.

Mirror, Mirror -- Do you have a go-to, make-you-feel-like-conquering-the- world kinda outfit? What do you like about it? If you don't have one, describe what you would include in your million-dollar outfit. What message would you like to send to your haters?

9-i

Invest in YOU!

Increase your knowledge! Read, ask questions, inquire, study, research, and ask more questions.

Before I talk about investing in key, quality clothing items that you can build a wardrobe around, the first thing to invest in is you! As with most things in life, what you put into it will be what you get out of it. If you plant good seeds in your garden of life, water them and keep the weeds out, then your garden will surely grow. Ask anyone who often tends to a garden and they will tell you, having a beautiful garden requires an investment of time, resources, and patience to reap the beauty of the bloom.

Invest in a few quality and classic clothing pieces that will stand the test of time, and will look great every time you wear them. Nothing lasts forever; things will go out of style, only to come back again. For example, the neon trend (we've seen that before), color block (been there, done that), animal print (here we go again), skinny jeans, wide leg jeans, high waist pants, chunky heels, platforms, nude lips, red lips, cat eye eyeliner, colorful nails, the list of trends goes on forever. But there is something to be said about having classic, well-made, attire that no matter what the trends, you will always be in style. These items may cost a little more at first, but, if you calculate the cost per wear, in the long run, you will get more bang for your buck. Here is a list of 11 pieces of clothing worth investing in:

- The LDB (little black dress): Choose a simple style that flatters your body type and that you can wear on multiple occasions. Choose a fabric that is not too shiny and not too casual so that you can add or subtract a wardrobe extender (i.e. cardigan, scarf or fun accessory) and make it fabulous!

- The tailored white dress shirt: Classic, chic (pronounced-sheek), and timeless. Select one that has a full-length sleeve and basic buttons, cuffed or uncuffed. This wardrobe staple never goes out of style. Wear it under a blazer or cardigan or under a vest for a different look altogether. The tailored white dress shirt is one of the most versatile pieces you can have in your closet; make it work for you. Make sure that you care for it properly (dry clean or wash and press) so that you can maximize the life of your garment.

- A cardigan sweater will add some pizazz to your wardrobe. Choose one that is the color of the season or one with a simple print. Not only will it keep you warm on chilly evenings and is easy to pack if traveling, but you can also wear it with the tailored white shirt we talked about above by tying it around your shoulders for a "look great without trying too hard" vibe.

- The- walk-five-miles-if-I-have-to-heels: This is one item that paying a little more for will pay for itself in the long run. Be sure to choose a pair of black pumps, preferably closed toe with a medium heel. A quality pair of pumps will feel and perform better on your feet. No matter how cute shoes are, if you can't walk in them because they are uncomfortable, it's not worth the purchase even if they are on sale.

- A pencil skirt can be one of the most useful items of clothing in a woman's wardrobe because it can be dressed up or down. Consider it a building block that will pair very nicely with the tailored white shirt, cardigan, and the walk-five-miles- if-I-have-to black pumps. These four items are the staples of a fabulous wardrobe!

- The perfect pair of jeans: think dark wash and great fit in boot cut or straight leg with at least 2% spandex for a better fit. This fabric mix also holds up better wash after wash. Swap out your pencil skirt and replace it with your super fabulous perfectly fitted jeans; keep the other items in place and you can transition to a casual event effortlessly. Every woman needs a pair of five pockets, straight leg jeans. They're classic, versatile, and flatter almost everybody's body type. The only place not to wear them would be a job interview or a black tie event unless otherwise specified in the invitation.

- The Blazer: If you want to dress to impress but a suit seems too formal, then a well-made blazer may be just what the fashion police won't ticket! This is one of my FAVORITE items! I have lots of blazers and jackets in my wardrobe. They can be an outfit dealmaker. They can be worn with your white dress shirt and cardigan for a layering effect; with the pencil skirt for the suit look or with the dark jeans for a casual Friday at your internship. Try a denim blazer, tweed, stripped for the men's wear-inspired look or even a tuxedo jacket for stepping up your game! Make sure it fits in the shoulders you can button it comfortably, and instantly, you are good to go almost anywhere.

- The tailored trouser: A good fitting pair of slacks can make your behind look firmer and your belly flatter; who couldn't love a pair of pants that can do that? Think of fabrics such as a wool or a poly blend. Opt for solid colors, black or grey, or a small sophisticated stripe. Switch out your pencil skirt or dark jeans with the cardigan and blazer and voila--changeroo, switcheroo better than a host at the MTV awards show!

- The belted trench coat: The November 1918 issue of a *Harper's Bazaar* magazine recommended the Trench coat as a gift for women serving in the armed forces. The price then was $ 65; almost a century later, the classic trench coat is still a fashionable wardrobe must have. Burberry's logoed trench coat begins around $ 1,200, yet if you wore yours on an average of twice a week for 50 years, your cost per wear would be about .25 cents; an unbeatable investment. Imagine the savings if your great grandmother had bought one back in 1918 and passed it down to you!

- Pearl earrings and necklace: They don't have to be oyster farmed but a simple, classic off-white pair always gives a classy look and feel. Pearls even when worn with a T-shirt give off a vibe of being classy and polished.
- A properly fitted bra that provides support and shape: Even though this is an item that won't be seen on the outside, it is perhaps one of the more important investments that you can make.

Most of these items can be purchased on a simple budget and can be replaced or updated with the latest looks as they become worn.

 *Mirror, Mirror -- Which one of the above key items do you already have in your closet? Which ones will you make a point to purchase in the near future? How can you invest in you starting now?*

increase your respect factor

What's in a name? It's not so much what you are called that matters but what you answer to that speaks volumes. We all are uniquely created from the top of our heads to the soles of our feet. This includes our names. I was recently listening to a sermon our pastor gave on how people were named in biblical times. He said that people were named based on what type of birth experience their mother had. He used the example of a biblical character Jabez, whose name meant sorrow, pain, and trouble. Thankfully in modern day, we are not as much named for the same reasons as Jabez.

My pastor's point was to live beyond the name we were given, because we are birthed into the world for greatness. We don't have any say in what we are named. Our parents are held accountable for that task; but we can control what we respond to. In today's music and entertainment industry, it troubles me to hear some of the names that our young ladies are being called; those names are far from what their parents named them. What is equally disturbing are the names that I hear us call each other. As seen on many of the popular reality shows, if a "cat fight" breaks out between the ladies --I use the term ladies very loosely in this case -- the first thing you hear is bleep, bleep, bleep followed by more name-calling and more bleeping. We are living in a time that appears to condone and accept being called names that are insulting, disrespectful, and downright wrong. We have a choice; demand respect in what we are called and more so what we answer to. Demand respect. PERIOD.

Ladies, if you follow the above advice and carry yourself in a way that doesn't compromise your integrity, then people will learn to respect you. Along the lines of what's in a name comes creating an email address. When creating an email address, keep it professional. Sometimes that is the first line of communication you have with someone. Having an email like babygirlphatcat@whatever.com sends a message before you press send. Such email addresses may be acceptable for communicating with friends, but when it comes to communicating with teachers, professionals or potential employers, having a professional email address is a good rule of thumb.

Mirror, Mirror -- What is your favorite TV reality show? Who are some of your favorite characters and why? Does it reflect YOUR reality?

J-j

Just because it's in the fashion magazines, your friends are wearing it, you find it on sale, and they have it on the rack in your size, does NOT mean that you have to have it in YOUR closet.

Justify basics over trends. Ask yourself can I wear it more than one season? Can I wear it to school or place of worship or to hang out? Is it in my budget to purchase? How will I care for the item? Is it properly made? These are questions that you need to ask yourself before you make a purchase. Tons of stores sell trendy accessory items that are fun and easy on the wallet. Trends usually last a season or two at the most, go away for a couple of years, and then reappear like we have never seen them before.

Magazines are a great place to spot trends before the seasons. The fashion industry is always a season or two ahead. Look at any fashion magazine to figure out what will be coming down the runways the next season. Trends and fashion inspiration come from lots of different origins. The key is to understand what works for you and what is best to leave on the runway. Fashion designers travel the world for inspiration to create the next item that will go from runway (think models strutting their stuff wearing the latest designs) to real world (how it will look on you and me).

just do the darn thing!

Many times when we are faced with a big task, it may appear to be too large to tackle. This is when we must put on our big girl panties and forget our F.E.A.R. A couple of acronyms for fear are (Forget Everything and Run or Face Everything and Rise).

But before you begin to tackle your challenges head on, let me ask you a related question: How do you eat an elephant? If you answered with hot sauce, that is not the right answer! Try one bite at a time. Big challenges don't have to throw you off your game, if you break them off in small bites. Before you know it, little by little you made it happen. I heard a saying once, that inch by inch it's a cinch, but yard by yard we make it hard! I too believe this. Your dreams need to be BIG enough to scare you...into giving it your all!

𝒦-𝓀

Know your body type

Are you apple, hourglass, rectangle, or pear shaped? Whatever type you are is beautiful: God made you this way on purpose. By knowing your body type you will be able to dress to accentuate (put on blast) the positive and camouflage the less than perfect things that you may not like about your body. The fit, fabric, and the designer of the garment will all play a huge part in the way an item fits on the body. One designer's size is not the same size as another's. Don't get caught up with the size on the label because all sizes are NOT created equally.

Buy what fits properly -- not too tight, not too short. When you bend, I don't want to see your foundational garments or worse. When you stretch, I don't want to see your stomach or worse. Refer to letter A - -**Always have a full-length mirror at the crib**! Do the in-store garment test before you leave the store. When trying on a garment, sit down in it, cross your legs in it, bend over in it. Think of it as a garment test-drive. It's easier to adjust sizes while still at the store than to have to return an item. But just in case, be familiar with the store's return and exchange policy. Try before you buy!

keep pictures of yourself in your favorite outfit and reference them on days when you need a little lovin' on you!

Ladies, this is really important: respect your temple! Showing too much skin, cleavage or back could send the wrong message.

Respect yourself and others will too! Social media outlets like Facebook and Instagram have made it easy for our lives to be open (face)books. Although Facebook, Instagram, Tumblr, Snapchat and Kik are wonderful social networking tools, please be careful what kind of photos and words you share with the world. Be mindful that potential employers may visit these sites to check out applicants. Make sure that your choice of photos and commentary are something that you would not be ashamed for potential employers, business contacts, school references or your mom to see. While we are on the subject of what not to share, like and what not to wear, here are some rules to remember when posting on social media.

Don't post:

- Personal information about yourself and your family.
- Information that would be sexually, racially, or politically offensive to others.
- Photos that show too much skin or show you and friends in compromising situations.
- Once it's out there in cyberspace, it's there forever!

A final thought: if you have to think twice (and you should) about posting it, it probably shouldn't be posted!

"Kool & Klassy" - When I was growing up, I lived on a street with girls about my age (Shout out to Darlene, Joli and Schadell!). We went to school together, went to church together, and played together. This was back in the day when baseball shirts were a popular item to wear; you had to come in when the street lights came on and the musical group *New Edition* had all the girls screaming! Most of you reading this may be too young to remember any of that; thank goodness!

We called ourselves the Kool & Klassy girls; yes, spelled with a K. We thought it would be fitting to get baseball shirts with our name and Kool & Klassy on them. We set out on a mission to save our money and bug our parents to get those shirts. We took pride in wearing them to events like skating parties and school dances. You couldn't tell us a thing, especially that we weren't what the shirts said, "Kool & Klassy." But it was more than just a shirt; it was an attitude and the way that we acted when we wore those shirts. Plus, we knew that all the parents in the neighborhood and the small town where we grew up could easily identify us. If we were not doing what we were supposed to be doing, word would get back to our parents quicker than we could make it back home!

Mirror, Mirror -- Your clothes speak before you are able to; what do they say? Would they mirror your thoughts? Would they speak in your voice? What makes you Kool & Klassy?

L-l

Love yourself first

The late, super-talented singer Whitney Houston made famous the song, "The Greatest Love of All." The lyrics are powerful and speak much truth. Love is the foundation of most good things and self-love is the foundation you need to build a beautiful and confident you. When you have self-love, you need not worry about what others think of you because the love you have for yourself will supersede (become more than) and be more powerful than any other love (with the exception of God's love).

Apply the four L's- love, look, listen, and learn - to your life. Love yourself, look inside yourself to understand and respect the person you are becoming; listen to that small voice inside; learn the lessons that come from the mistakes you make and continue on your path to lifelong learning!

less is more. Quality over quantity is the way to go.

Take it from me, it's very easy to get carried away with buying items just because they are on sale! Who really needs 12 black T-shirts? You don't unless they are a part of a uniform that you wear daily. I have found that even though I may have 12 black T-shirts, I have about two that I wear most often. My point is if you purchase quality items that are well made you only need a few to incorporate into your wardrobe. The others are just taking up precious space in my closet! It may also be helpful to do a closet inventory. Go through and see what you have, see what you need and shop accordingly. Less is more can apply to other aspects of your life as well, like spending quality time with family and friends and less time texting, or more time studying and less time texting. You get the point!

M-m

Makeover your attitude

No one wants to be around someone who is negative, puts other people down, never has a kind word to say about anyone or anything, and drinks hateraide on constant rotation.

Hateraide, as defined by the Urban Dictionary: "When a person or group of unsuccessful people can't stop hating on someone who's wealthier, more successful and better than they are in every imaginable way."

Have you heard the saying that birds of a feather flock together? People who think and act alike are usually found in the same circles. There is nothing wrong with having friends in your circle who have similar interests; but, when a group of negative chicks get together, surely there is going to be less than positive comments. Many times if we can stop negative thoughts at their source, we can stop them from showing up and showing out! I used to tell my kids, "Put your brain on pause." If they couldn't think it, they couldn't say it!

Many years ago, I was in a workshop and the facilitator gave us an exercise to try. Each time you had a negative thought, you had to start over with that thought process. This is a harder task than you can imagine. It was an exercise in making over your thought process and creating positive thoughts over negative thoughts. Give that exercise a try right now. Not easy, huh? Practice makes perfect; the more you do it, the more positive your results. While on the exercise of creating a positive thought process, try this one, too. Spend six months minding your own business and worrying about yourself and the other six months not worrying about someone else. That's a whole year of taking care of you!

Way back when smallpox, a disease caused by a virus, caused facial disfigurement, refined ladies would fill in the pocks with beeswax. But when the weather was very warm, the wax would melt. But it was not acceptable for one lady to tell another that her makeup needed attention. Hence the phrase, "Mind your own beeswax!" (aka check yourself!)

"A pretty face means nothing if the person wearing it has an ugly attitude."-- Unknown

money -- The amount of money you spend on clothes and material items can't make you look better IF your attitude isn't right. (re-read above)

Don't be a **Magnet Girl.**

A former coworker and I named a colleague "Magnet Girl" because it seemed like she stepped into a dark closet each morning with an industrial-size magnet, and whatever stuck to the magnet is what she wore that day. We were amazed at the combination of things that she put together.

I have a saying: Have only one -- never over two -- "star" pieces per outfit. When I look at you, I shouldn't have to figure out what item is the focal point of your outfit; if you have on a fabulous necklace, there may not be a need to have on an equally fabulous belt and shoes and earrings in the same ensemble. If you choose the necklace as "the statement piece," it can be the "wow factor!" If you have too much going on, it can be a disaster. Too much of a good thing can be bad!

𝓝-𝓷

Never give up on your dreams

We hear the phrase dress for success a lot, but what does it really mean? I think that dressing for success has to do with presenting yourself in a positive and professional manner that results in you looking and feeling confident. Dressing for success also has to do with being appropriate for the occasion. Many times we hear dress for success relative to the professional arena. But dressing for success applies to other areas of our lives as well.

I have always had a passion for fashion and what better way to honor that passion than to start a Dress for Success affiliate in my community. Dress for Success is a national non-profit organization that gives women the appropriate attire and skills to help them obtain and retain employment with the ultimate goal of becoming self-sufficient. Everyone needs to have a dream and sometimes you may be the only person who believes in your dream, and that's okay. Dream on anyhow!

When I started doing research on Dress for Success in the early 2000's, I contacted the office in New York about how to get started. I was told that someone had already expressed interest in starting an affiliate chapter in Winston-Salem, N.C., so they recommended that I work with them in this effort. I reached out to that person and was elated that I found someone who shared my passion of helping women so I thought. When she and I met, I shared my ideas with her. I had a gut feeling that something was not right with the partnership, but I couldn't put my finger on it. I soon realized that her heart was not in it for the right reasons.

She took my ideas, used them as her own, and left me with my broken dreams in the dust. I was angry, sad, disappointed, and hurt, just to name a few of the emotions I was feeling. I tucked my dream way in the back of my mind and went on with life. I thought about it from time to time but convinced myself that it just wasn't the right time to pursue my dream. The funny thing is my "business partner" ended up dropping the ball on the work that "we" had done.

Fast forward to 2007 when I saw a magazine article on Dress for Success; the new CEO was Joi Gordon. Reading that article gave me the motivation that I needed to dust off my dreams and try again. I emailed Joi the next day; in her response she said, "I am so glad that you didn't give up on your dreams!" Those words were what I needed to hear to get back in the game to complete my assignment. After many years of hard work, sacrifice, and prayer, in March 2010, we received the non-profit charter for Dress for Success Winston-Salem.

I share my story to encourage you to NEVER give up on your dreams. In time, all things will work together for the good of those that believe their dreams CAN come true!

naturally done makeup and nails are often just enough.

Recently I did some trend surveying at one of my favorite shopping spots. The young clerk at the checkout counter had red, yellow, and blue braids in her hair and long multi-colored fingernails. When I saw her, I shook my head wondering, who let her out of the house looking like that? With all of the new developments in makeup and hair coloring, multicolored hair and nails are becoming a style or preference; a.k.a trend. But not always a good trend. Let me say for the record, that I have **nothing** against self-expression; however, you will hear me say that there is a time and a place for all things and if someone has to wonder what statement your hair and nails are trying to make, **it** may be time for an intervention!

"Your inner beauty never needs makeup." (Pinterest Quote)

Mirror, Mirror -- Do you have a passion for something and you love it enough to do it without getting paid?

O-o

Overcome obstacles one at a time

I mentioned earlier in the book how you can eat a whole elephant one bite at a time. (hot sauce optional) This saying may sound a little strange but what that means is you can overcome obstacles by taking one step at a time to find a solution. Don't feel like you have to figure things out alone; go to your school's guidance counselor, a parent, trusted family member or friend. They can help you to overcome obstacles.

outerwear-make it a part of your overall look

Jackets, blazers, and trench coats are all useful garments that keep us warm and dry, but who says your clothes can't be fashionable *and* functional? A great coat can be your statement piece. If it looks great, it's the first thing that people see. Depending on the occasion, if you don't have to take it off, you won't have to worry about what you're wearing underneath! (it's always best to be prepared however, just in case!) But just as I mentioned earlier in the book that having a foundation garment wardrobe is important, so is having an outerwear wardrobe.

My kids like to wear hoodies...EVERYWHERE. Hoodies are not appropriate to wear everywhere. To school perhaps and hanging out with friends, but depending on the weather and the occasion, you may need an alternate option for outerwear. Yes, it may seem like a waste of money if you only wear it a limited amount of time, however, these items can be purchased on sale, at the end of the season or a discount retail store.

For you never know when the occasion may call for you to wear a nice dress, cute pumps and pearls and a hoodie on top may not be the most appropriate icing on the cake. Challenge yourself to step up your style game and play to win!

𝒫-𝓅

Perception is NOT always reality

I was at a birthday celebration and saw a young sister who was well endowed on the backside. She had on black stretch pants that revealed her very large bottom, butt, rear, badonkadonk, junk in the trunk! But her waist was not large in comparison to her posterior. (aka buttocks) I wondered if it was challenging for her to find clothing to fit and flatter her figure. I also wondered if she was at all affected by the attention that she may receive because of the way God created her body. Was she self-conscious about it? Do her family and friends love and accept her just the way she is? Was it even a non-issue because not even exercise would change the size of her bottom? This led me to a history lesson that I shared with my husband and daughter.

Sarartjee (Sara) Baartmann, nicknamed Hottentot Venus, was born in 1789 as a slave in the Khoi Khoi Tribe in South Africa. She was born with distinct features including oversized buttocks and other abnormal physical features that made her "famous." At age 20, she was put on display in the Piccadilly Circus and other sideshows where people paid money to see her body. Her's was a life filled with loneliness, shame and ridicule. Even after her death, her skeleton and other body parts remained on display at a museum in Paris.

Finally after much debate and plight for justice over her radical exploitation for others' entertainment purposes, she was given a proper burial more than 200 years after her birth. In researching this

46

interesting topic, I came to find out that although Sara Baartman may have become famous for the features that she was born with and spent a lifetime being ridiculed for there are others who make it a choice to embrace and love their bodies.

In a November 2014 article for the London Daily Mail, I came across a story of another woman, age 39, whose hip spam spreads to 8 feet. In an internet article, she said that she started experiencing expansion after her first child was born. She is married with three children and has a wonderful and supportive husband. She says that she is healthy and that she loves her body. She recalls instances when she hears onlookers negative and rude remarks as she walks down the street and hears the snapping of photos with their cell phones. She said that she rises above that and hopes to inspire women to think, "She's happy with her body and I can be, too."

I find it amazing that some celebs have paid to have their butts shaped like that of Sara Baartman. Not only in the celebrity world is there the desire to enlarge and enhance certain body features, but women are even going to the extremes of butt pumping which has also become a popular and deadly practice. Butt pumping is when an unlicensed person injects a mixture of silicone, mineral oil and fix-a-flat, a product used to temporarily inflate a flat tire, into another person's body. Not only is this illegal, but it is also deadly. My point is this…God made you just the way he wants you to be.

"Don't be ashamed of the way you look. You have exactly what somebody else wants."-- (Pinterest quote)

Mirror, Mirror -- What is your most flattering feature? What one thing would you change if you could and why? What beauty enhancements would you consider trying and why?

Put your best foot forward. But six-inch heels or flip-flops may NOT be the answer!

Stilettos and platform heels are all great shoe options for the right time and the right place. Daily wear of high heels can lead to ingrown toenails, sprained ankles, bunions, heel spurs, and overall **bad** feet as you grow older. Trust what I am telling you!

I was on the campus of Winston-Salem State University, my undergraduate alma mater, and noticed that many of the young women were wearing high heels across campus. I watched as they maneuvered sidewalks and steps, a task for the skilled, as they rushed to class. I was in awe but I was also in pain just to watch! Research has linked the wearing of high heels in youth to heel and ankle pain in older adults. Just as high heels may cause challenges, on the low side, flip-flops have little to no support for the feet.

Speaking of flips that flopped, in 2005 the Northwestern University Women's lacrosse team visited the White House. In a picture with President George W. Bush, four of the nine champions pictured on the front row were wearing flip-flops. The picture sparked a mini controversy on whether it was appropriate to wear flip-flops for a visit to the White House. A July 2005 front-page story in the *Chicago Tribune* read, "YOU WORE FLIP FLOPS TO THE WHITE HOUSE?!" The article was inspired by an email from one of the player's older brothers.

One of the player's mothers said, "She was mortified!" A team member argued that they weren't just any old flip-flops – that these flip-flops had rhinestones on them and cost $ 16. Another team member said that she considered them a dressier version of a sandal. After the controversy, the team members decided to auction the shoes to benefit a charity campaign for a little girl with a brain tumor. While wearing flip flops may not be appropriate for the occasion, wearing six-inch heels may not be appropriate either.

Recently, I was watching videos of high school graduations and several of the young female graduates were wearing very high heels, one stumbled across the graduation stage and fell as she tried without success to steady herself. There are many kinds of shoes ranging from ballerina flats to wedges and cute kitten heels that are fashionable, comfortable, and perfect for any outfit. Just make sure that they will be appropriate and comfortable for whatever the occasion. Falling is NOT fashionable!

Podiatrists recommend in a May 2015 Live Science online article that women limit their time in heels and flip-flops when they will be walking or standing for long periods. It also suggested that women outline their feet on inflexible cardboard and take the cut out with them when going shoe shopping. If the cardboard can't fit into the shoe without being scrunched, neither can your feet. Protect and love your feet and they will support you for a long time to come! But remember to use your better judgment and a big dose of common sense; if you are not sure that something is appropriate for the occasion, ask a mentor for advice.

"Shoes speak louder than words."-- Unknown

Personal Brand = Y.O.U.—You are your own personal brand. I read this on Facebook and it pretty much says it all. Your smile is your logo, your personality is your business card, how you leave others feeling after having an experience with you becomes your trademark. Personal branding includes your personality, the way you dress, your handshake, and the way you communicate with others. It defines who you are and how you come across to others. When I think about branding, designer brands like Nike and stores like Aeropostale come to mind. These companies create a brand message in the way they design their garments, labels, logos, packaging, and displays. Whenever you see these brands, you automatically know who that designer is or what that store carries.

With our favorite restaurants, even if we don't see the actual store, for example, the "Golden Arches," you always know that's McDonald's. Branding is what helps market and ultimately sell a product. We are all our own best sales associates for our personal brand.

I remember hearing someone say, "Nothing happens in the world until something is bought or sold." One could say sales help make the world go 'round. Well, before you can become successful, you have to sell *yourself*. Not in terms of a red price sticker on your forehead and displayed in a storefront window...but close. Because each of us is a brand, before we are able to sell ourselves to the world, we have to polish our brand and make sure that it's ready for the marketplace. Your brand deserves to be sold in the very best, upscale and exclusive stores. No flea markets or bargain basement mentality here!

If you are not being treated with the love and respect that you deserve, check your "PRICE TAG." Perhaps you've marked yourself down. It's YOU that determines what you are worth by what you accept. Get off the CLEARANCE RACK and get behind the glass case where valuables are kept. **Bottom line, value yourself more.**

"If you're searching for that one person that will change your life, take a look in the mirror."--Roman Price, Founder of LifePulp, social media specialist, part-time superhero and life enthusiast.

Mirror, Mirror -- What does your brand say about you? Create a slogan for your brand. What is it and what is your best selling feature? What sets your brand apart from others?

2-q

Question it if it doesn't feel right

Peer pressure, bullying, sexting, inappropriate advances, whatever the case, if you are uncomfortable with it, **speak up**! Tell someone that you trust to help you. Ladies, **never** think that you have to put up with improper treatment, inappropriate advances or abuse. Even if a teacher or coach that you trust does something that makes you uncomfortable, don't think you have to put up with it or be silenced because of fear. NO ONE has the right to take advantage of you! Protect yourself and be aware of your surroundings and your "friends," including people that you meet through social media. Just because you can't physically see them doesn't mean that you don't need to be careful with the information that you share with them. It's always better to be safe than sorry when it comes to taking care of and protecting yourself. It it doesn't feel right, reach out for help!

queen mentality

You need to have it! I love Queen Latifah (Latifah in Arabic means delicate and very kind). She is a rapper, actress, talk show host, cosmetic and fragrance model and all-around cool chick. She appeared on the scene in 1989 as one of the first female rap artists, paving the way for many female artists on the scene today. Latifah's song "Ladies First" empowers women and makes them proud to be women. She demanded respect on the stage as well as off. So a queen by definition is a female ruler of an independent state, who behaves in a pleasant and superior manner, reigns on her own behalf and is in charge! Check out "Ladies First" on YouTube.

Ask a Queen

I had the pleasure of meeting a real queen, Ms. Nadia Shirin Moffitt, Ms. North Carolina USA 2010. This is what she had to say about being a queen:

> Glynis-What is your definition of a queen and what makes her tiara sparkle?
>
> Nadia-A woman who knows who she is in all aspects of her life. She has talents and gifts to share with the world. She is a woman of success and her brand makes her unique and different to inspire others with her actions. She starts with herself.
>
> Glynis-What is The Queen's Foundation and what inspired you to start it?
>
> Nadia-The Queen's Foundation is a non-profit organization that leads under-served middle and high school young women in North Carolina to life transformation so they can be the generation of change. I started the organization to build Queen's starting with herself and to build a strong foundational structure. This impacts their families and the world. This all starts with our girls.
>
> Glynis-What advice would you give queens about reigning supreme on the throne of life?
>
> Nadia-Never, ever, ever, ever, ever give up. When you decide on something for your life, go hard for

it. Look at everything in your life as a sign and it will bring you closer to identifying the purpose for your life!

"Think like a queen. A queen is not afraid to fail. Failure is another steppingstone to greatness."-- Oprah Winfrey, American media mogul, famous talk show host, actress, producer and world-class philanthropist.

Mirror, Mirror -- Who do you consider a queen in your life and why? What are some of the queen qualities that she possesses? Do you consider yourself a queen? If so, what queen qualities do you possess?

R-r

Realize your full potential and reach out for help

This is where role models can make a big difference in your life! My mother, grandmothers, aunts, some school teachers and community leaders were and still are great role models to me. They were women (and men) that I looked up to, admired, and respected. We all need someone to help us get through the challenges that life will present and to encourage us to be our best. Perhaps it's a teacher, or coach, someone in your church or community that could serve as your role model or mentor.

In addition to having role models in my family and community, I look up to the First Lady of the United States, Michelle Obama. I marvel at the way she carries herself. She appears to be down to earth and real whether she is rocking a designer gown or a dress from Target. She makes it work for her. She's classy, smart, and always looks well-dressed no matter the occasion.

Narcisco Rodriguez is a fashion designer who specializes in women's formalwear. He worked with First Lady Obama and had this to say about her style: "I see her as an inspiration. She's intoxicating. As a role model and woman of style, I think she's so incredibly beautiful. She is so unapologetic about her personal style and what she likes. She wears all of it with such dignity and grace. I love that fashion doesn't define her, but she loves it so much and it's such a big part of her life. And that's how it should be!"

Really... you're going to wear that?

Realize your best assets and make them shine. Size matters. You've heard that saying? I interpret it as, buy what fits YOU best. I see far too many body rolls, muffin tops, cleavage, and thong imprints, much of which is attributed to buying the wrong size. Just like age is just a number, so is size. If you are going to make the effort to buy an item, buy it to fit. Don't look at the size; look at how you look and feel in the item.

Ratchet Revisited-The Remix

Because I have teenagers in my house, I am introduced to some pretty interesting things by way of social media. I am glad they share some of those things with me as it gives me a glimpse into what they are seeing and hearing. One day my daughter was talking about someone at her school being ratchet. When I asked her what she was talking about, she pulled up the most interesting and entertaining video on YouTube.

Two brothers, the Hudson Brothers, had done a skit to bring ratchet to life. Ratchet as defined by the Merriam Webster dictionary as "a mechanism consisting of a prawn that engages the sloping teeth of a wheel or bar." However, the Urban Dictionary defines "Ratcheet," an adjective meaning, "is a person who is nasty, ghetto, or trifling." Since my original introduction to ractcheet, I have seen many examples of it live and in person! So much of what we call ourselves comes from slang and street definitions that someone else coined.

The fact of the matter is we don't have to own, attach ourselves to, allow anyone to call us, or believe that we are ratcheet or any other term of the sort. What we think about, we bring about. This is why we have to be very careful to understand what we are **not**! There is power in the tongue and things said even in jest or jokingly can end up sticking without us even being aware of it.

Speaking of ratcheet brings me to another R-Reality TV! With so much reality TV, studies have found that 72 percent of tween and teen girls who view these type programs say they spend more time on their appearance, while only 42 percent of non-viewers agreed. Who hasn't gotten caught up with a reality TV show every now and then? However, when our TV viewing consumption starts to affect the image of ourselves based on what someone else thinks, looks or feels, it may be time to take a closer look at what impression -- sometimes lasting -- these shows may have on our influential minds.

Much of reality TV is far from our known reality. In some shows, we may find something we can relate to relate to. But much of what we see has been doctored for TV so that we will watch. Money, cars, fast fame, ridiculous consumption of material items and careless regard for people in general are so much of what reality TV is made of. If we watch enough of it, we too may acquire some of its offenses.

You may have heard the saying, "Truth is stranger than fiction." Your life may not be perfect, but it's yours and what you make of it is up to you. The image of some of these reality TV "stars"-- I use the term star very loosely -- is not at all flattering or nice for that matter. No matter how much money you have, if you don't love yourself and are unable to love your neighbor, then it is not worth the paper that it is printed on. In ten years, we will barely remember these reality show "stars" who are currently household names.

S-s

Self-Esteem affects the way we dress

Do you know that there is a correlation with clothing and how it impacts the way a person feels? Do you know someone who wears dark colors most of the time? Do you notice that they may also have a dark attitude to mirror their clothing color choices? Or that people who take a chance with color act with a colorful attitude? It's true. Our clothing choices and the colors that we choose are a direct reflection of our self-esteem. The Merriam Webster dictionary defines self-esteem as having confidence and satisfaction in oneself.

I love this quote: "If you're wearing a disguise for too long, it will be difficult for the mirror to recognize you. At the end of the day, I hope you become the person they didn't expect you to be. Be proud to wear you." -- Dodinsky, New York Times best selling author.

Our clothing is an extension of who we are. And it reflects how we feel, what mood we are in, if we are happy or sad and even if we are approachable. Clothing speaks its own language, one that sometimes not even we understand. I truly believe that "dressing up" can instantly improve one's attitude and self-esteem. I witnessed success stories often when I worked with the wonderful women that we served at our Dress for Success Winston-Salem program. Oftentimes a client would visit us feeling frustrated with where they were in life; she may have had her head hung low and may have been a little sad. However, when she put on a suit, pumps, and some jewelry, an instant transformation happened; she walked a little taller, held her head a little higher, and most often, I saw a beautiful smile spread across her lips. I truly feel it has something to do with enhancing her dress. No, this doesn't always change a person's situation, but positive transformation often starts with a look. Building confidence from the outside in.

In an April 2012 article from the *New York Times*, research revealed the effects certain types of clothing have on the mindset of the wearer. It pointed out that, "Clothes invade the body and brain, putting the wearer into a different psychological state." The article went on to say: It has long been known that "clothing affects how other people perceive us as well as how we think about ourselves," Dr. Adam D. Galinsky said. Other experiments have shown that women who dress in a masculine fashion during a job interview are more likely to be hired, and a teaching assistant who wears formal clothes is perceived as more intelligent than one who dresses more casually.

My interpretation -- if you dress for success physically then psychologically you are closer to becoming successful.

shop in your own closet first before hitting the malls

We've all been guilty of thinking that we NEED a new outfit to wear to that next big event coming up on our busy social calendar, however resist the urge and shop in your closet, there are more than likely a few hidden treasures. In case you may not know by now, I LOVE to shop! (Shocked face) It never fails that I will discover a hidden treasure at the back of my closet. This is especially true at the beginning of each season. Inevitably, I will find an item on sale at the end of the season, and I will pack it away until time to use it. Of course, I had forgotten about it. So when I see it again, I'm excited and can't wait to rock it!

However, there is a downside to these end-of-the-season items too-good-to-pass-up, I-can't-wait-to-wear bargains. Often, I end up with more black T-shirts than I need. The key to successful wardrobe planning and management is knowing what you have, knowing what you need, knowing where to find them, and knowing when to buy them. Remember dress to impress you, not others! Do you first boo!

Style, I love that word!

To me, it conjures up visions of runways and designer labels, models and couture (koo too r) catwalks. But it also reminds me of the lady who knows what works well for her, shops wisely and takes pride dressing to impress herself first. I believe that style is nothing until you make it your own. That is why everyone should have a signature style that they cultivate. I have several signature styles, but my favorite is wearing a flower pin on my lapel. When admirers compliment me on my pin, I tell them I am growing where I am planted. Think about that — we grow where we are planted. I may not be where I want to be or where I will ultimately end up in life, but for that moment I am blooming and brightening the soil that I am in.

For others, their signature style may be a strand of pearls, red lipstick, hoop earrings or a signature haircut. Whatever the signature style you choose to create, own it and have fun with it. Your signature style may change as you do -- for the better!

"Insist on being true to yourself. Be your own style, your way." -- Jennifer Gayle, Australian actress and model.

Mirror, Mirror -- What's your signature style? How do you make it work for you?

Style Guide 101

Wouldn't it be great if each invitation we received came with a magic wand and our own personal fashion stylist? That would certainly assist with being appropriately attired for whatever the occasion. But since that's usually never the case, we may see attire that includes everything from diamonds to denim. There are some simple rules to follow to insure that you are dressed appropriately, comfortably, and ready for fun. Consider these things before deciding what to wear: time of day, place of event, cultural influences, dress code and if you're playing a special role. Please make sure you RSVP (Répondez S'il Vous Plaît) if the invitation requests and be mindful of the deadline to do so!

- Black Tie -- Formal (for evening events) proms, galas, award ceremonies, very special occasions. Note to self: It's **always** better to be overdressed than underdressed.

Pull out all the stops! This is one of the few times in life that wearing a full- length gown is the way to go. I have loved playing dress up for as long as I can remember — from proms, to the Miss Teen North Carolina pageant, to the first runner-up as college queen as Miss Winston-Salem State University. I also won the title as Miss Alpha Phi Alpha representing a college fraternity. I had lots of formal wear, so much so, that my mom said that she was not going to buy me another formal dress until it was time to buy my wedding gown. In fact, I wanted to wear a white tails tuxedo complete with top hat and cane to my senior prom. That idea didn't go over too well with my date, so I opted for a lavender lace dress instead!

This is the appropriate time to think dressy, festive, elegant and classy with heels and the cutest little clutch that you can find to hold your keys, lip gloss, phone, tissues, and your identification. In the days before cell phones, my mother used to say, "Take a quarter in case you need to use the payphone." How many of you have ever seen a payphone?

- Semi -- formal, After Five, cocktail dress, dinner parties, fancy parties.

Think knee-length dress; not too short. Sequins are really in now and are not just for evenings. With this category of dress, sequins are a perfect choice, even in small doses. You may want to also consider a dress that has details or texture. This is where a LBD (Little Black Dress) can be a girl's best friend. Just add a splash of color to your LBD with your accessories, shoes and clutch, and you are on your way to get the party started!

- Business Casual -- work, work-related events, meetings, seminars.

In the United States, at 43 percent of non-self-employed workers commonly wear casual business attire. Casual street wear is the next most common work attire at 28 percent, closely followed by uniforms at 19 percent. Only a minority of workers, 9 percent, wear formal business attire.

This is where I spend a lot of time talking about how to dress for success! Of course, such talks depend on what type of work you are doing and what your work environment dictates as a dress code. Being appropriately dressed for work can mean the difference between a promotion and a pink slip! If your workplace calls for a uniform, then make sure it is clean, wrinkle free, and that you have all the required pieces. Do your homework before you go on an internship or job shadowing opportunity. This is also the case if you are interviewing for a position with a company. Never make assumptions about the dress code. Even if the dress code for the workplace allows jeans, they are not appropriate for the interview. Remember to always make a great first impression!

- Dressy or business casual -- school or work events, social events, networking events.

The Merriam Webster dictionary defines casual as being without ceremony or formality; relaxed: *a casual evening with friends.* Suited for everyday wear or use; informal. Add dressy in front of the casual and this calls for a blazer or jacket with a skirt or nice khakis, no spaghetti straps or too much skin showing. This is a time to get creative and have a little fun with your wardrobe choices. Being appropriate doesn't mean boring!

- Casual -- weekends, hanging out with friends, non-business, vacation time.

This is a time to wear khakis or "good" jeans. A polo shirt or T-shirt, a sundress or maxi dress and sandals. This is the most laid-back style of dress appropriate for wear in public settings. The key with any of the above is to know the purpose of the occasion, what the activities will be and if there was a dress code stated by the hostess or in the invitation. Always keep in mind that you never know who you may meet so be dressed at your personal best at all times!

Dr. Linda Przybyszewski, (Dr. P.) who teaches at the University of Notre Dame in Indiana, wrote a book titled *The Lost Art of Dress.* Dr. P was featured on "ABC Good Morning America" Sunday Morning program. She also teaches a class, A Nation of Slobs. Being an advocate of appropriate dress, I was intrigued that we shared the same passion for proper dress. She says that "proper dress used to be so important. It was taught in school from first grade through college. And baring all, she says, is not "an artistic ideal." Professor P. sews many of her own clothes because dresses with beautiful details -- like sleeves with six-button cuffs -- are hard to find, she says.

"Anyone can get dressed up and glamorous but it is how
people dress in their days off that are the most intriguing."
-- Alexander Wang, famous american designer

Mirror, Mirror -- Do you think America is becoming a nation of slobs? Would you take a course of this subject matter like the one Professor P. teaches? Why or Why not?

I was recently in a chain discount store that I love to frequent. I proceeded to the check out; the cashier that helped me was young and probably working there for a summer job. She was very nice and had a great smile. However, I saw that she was wearing jean shorts and a T-shirt. Although it was a name brand T-shirt, I was baffled because she was wearing shorts and a T-shirt *at work*. It looked like she may have been going to hang out with some friends at the movies or staying at home watching TV, but NOT at work. I thought perhaps that the store was having a dress down day for employees. Giving her the benefit of the doubt, I thought of all the reasons that she decided to come to work dressed down. I am not saying that she had to have on tailor- made dress slacks, a collared shirt, and a pinstriped blazer; however, I am saying dress for the job that you want to have and keep. Although the job may be just for the summer, it makes sense to look at it as a possible future job opportunity or source for a reference. My point is this: people notice how you present yourself. If you present yourself in a casual manner, people will treat you in a casual way. Step up your game and dress for your next big break! There is a time and a place for T-shirts and jeans. They have long been a dynamic duo and can be found in most closets. The two can be dressed up and dressed down. Take note of the interesting history of the Batman (jeans) and Robin (T-shirt) of fashion.

Denim can be a wardrobe staple and is also known as britches, dungaree and trousers. Jeans made from denim, a cotton fabric, were first invented in the 1950's and were originally worn by cowboys and sailors, according to Prime Magazine.com. And at the time only came in a basic blue. Brands such as Levi's were among the original front runner in the jean category and set the stage for jeans as we know them today. Jeans have come a very long way in terms of wash, (acid, stone, dirty) style (skinny, flare, boot cut) and cost — costing from the cheapest ($ 1.50) to the most expensive pair ($ 1.3 million) commercially available according to therichest.com, a website featuring the 10 most expensive jeans. Most of us have at least one pair in our wardrobe; some may have over a dozen pairs. According to the Shopaholic's Daily Calendar 2012, even though we can only wear one pair at a time, the average woman owns ten pairs of jeans but wears on average only three of those pairs. Jeans, for most people, are a wardrobe staple and go with everything from a basic T-shirt to a tuxedo jacket. They were originally designed as casual wear but have taken on a lifestyle all their own. However, despite their mass popularity or the cost, they are not appropriate to wear everywhere. It is also the one item that can be worn the worst ways -- too tight, the wrong style for your body type, sagging, and deconstructed.

Denim, if done correctly, can be a fun and versatile item to incorporate into your wardrobe. There can also be what I call the fashion dangers of denim. These range from wearing head to toe denim, two or more shades in the same ensemble and over embellished. Too much of anything can turn out bad! I would recommend having three pair of jeans in your wardrobe arsenal, a skinny, a dark wash and another well-fitting pair of your choice. The next time that you go into your closet and reach for a pair of jeans, replace them with another choice, perhaps a pair of khakis or a skirt. If you wear jeans on a daily basis, try to do an upgrade outfit once a week and see what kind of outfits that you can create. Make it fun….fashion should be fun!

Along with jeans comes its partner in crime; the T-shirt. A T-shirt and a pair of well-fitting jeans can make a million and one outfits. According to Wikipedia, T-shirts surfaced in the United States when issued by the US Navy. They were the crew-neck style shirts worn as underwear beneath uniforms. Soon it was adopted by the Army as a part of the standard-issued ensemble given to recruits. Dock workers, farmers and construction-type workers also adopted the T-shirt preferring the lightweight fabric in hotter weather conditions. The most expensive T-shirt on record in the US cost $ 400,000 and takes 4 weeks to make and comes with a 1-year warranty!

I have seen lots of graphic print tees with interesting references and slogans. The earliest printed T-shirt dates back to the 1960's. T-shirts and their slogans have certainly changed over the years. Be careful about the messages that you portray through your choice of T-shirts. We attract what we project, so if we send a message based on the T-shirt we are wearing, be prepared for what you may attract. There is nothing worse, in my opinion, than a T-shirt with "baby girl" written across the front, but its 3 sizes too tight.

Sunday Best

I heard a comedian say that things have surely changed when a club has a dress code but the church says come as you are. In my opinion, come as you are has gone too far! I grew up in a small Baptist church in Hillsborough, North Carolina. It was the one place that you were expected to be on your best behavior unless you wanted to really get it when you got home! I remember one of the elders in our church, Ms. Gattis, always prayed this prayer: "We are not here for any outside show." I eventually came to understand what she was saying. That goes along the same lines as come just as you are, which means that you don't have to have the finest clothes, biggest hat and blingingist jewels to come to the church; come with what you have, and Jesus will meet you right where you are. I too believe in coming just as you are. But I feel the church is a sacred place and a certain amount of respect for God, oneself and others should be taken into consideration when entering God's house. This includes how we dress.

Some of the choices of attire that I have observed in church have left me speechless. Too short, too much skin, very high heels; I can't tell whether they are in church or in the club. As our sister's keepers, one of the best places to start shaping our future young ladies with love, faith, and guidance is in the church. I think about "Sunday Best," the reality TV show that finds the next up-and-coming gospel talent star. The show challenges contestants to perform their very best, and their goal is to win the prize — the recording contract. Perhaps, we should adopt the mentality to be at our personal Sunday Best in our dress, in the way we act, in the way we treat others **everyday** of the week! Here is a biblical reference that puts this all in perspective:

> Likewise also that women should adorn themselves in respectable apparel, with modesty and self-control, not with braided hair and gold or pearls or costly attire, but with what is proper for women who profess godliness — with good works.

> 1 Timothy 2:9-10

> Put YOUR Sunday Best to the Test!

Mirror, Mirror -- How can you put your Sunday Best to the test? Do you think that there should be "dress codes" for venues such as school, places of worship or social venues like the club?

T-t

Tough times don't last, tough people do!

Tenacity is the quality or fact of continuing to exist, persist and be determined. Here is an example: She practices her gymnastics routine with the tenacity of a bull dog. Think of a marathon runner, or Olympic swimmer or WNBA point guard. An example is Gabrielle Douglas, the US Women's artistic gymnast who won two Gold Medals in both team and individual competitions in 2012. She is the first woman of color of any nationality and the first African American gymnast in Olympic history to become the individual all around champion. Gabby is also the first American gymnast to win gold in both the gymnastic individual all around and the team competition at the same Olympic games. WOW, Gabby is the bomb! In order to be the best, it takes tenacity to condition your mind and your body for the task. You can't just *think* that you're the best. In order to *be* the best, you have to put in the time and the work. It takes hours of practice and dedication even on those days when you are tired and don't think that you can do it. You have to find the strength to make it happen.

too much of anything is not good

I always say have one focal-point piece per outfit. Too much of even a good thing can look bad. Every year, I purchase my favorite page-a-day calendar, "The Shopaholics Daily Calendar." Each day the calendar has tips and tricks for us shopaholics. The calendar also contains wonderful factoids that you can tuck away in your brilliant mind to incorporate into your next conversation that is sure to impress the hearer. I found this advice on one of the calendars — "Celeb Advice: It's always one amazing item that draws your attention. When you wear a lot of cool things at once, it's overkill!" I couldn't agree more!

𝒰-u

Uncover a beautiful you

You may have heard the expression, "a diamond in the rough." According to the Merriam Webster dictionary, that means "someone or something that has hidden exceptional characteristics and/or future potential, but currently lacks the final touches that would make them truly stand out from the crowd." The metaphorical definition relates to the fact that naturally occurring diamonds are quite ordinary at first glance, and their true beauty as jewels is only realized through the cutting and polishing process.

WOW that says so much about our inner beauty that we often don't realize we have. Just as we uncover beauty within ourselves, we can also discover and uncover what treasures that can be found at local thrift and consignment stores. I **love** shopping at thrift stores. I have found amazing items that I enjoy wearing. I smile to myself when someone pays me a compliment because only I know what a steal of a deal it was!

Many items are new with tags still on them from stores where I would never pay full prices. Looking fabulous doesn't have to break your bank. Be open to shopping at alternative places that can help you remain unique and can save you money at the same time — plus you may have a little fun discovering a hidden treasure. One of my favorite hidden treasure finds was from Tracy Reese, an African American designer. I have long admired her craft and talent as a designer but never thought that I would be able to purchase any of her designs. One day while thrifting in one of my favorite thrift stores, I came across a Tracy Reese dress. It still had the original tags on it from an upscale retailer. I was so excited that I was able to snag a designer piece at a fraction of the cost! But when I wore that dress, I wore it like I bought it full price hot off the designer's showroom floor!

Another hidden thrifting treasure is the Salvation Army Thrift Store. The specials change daily. The deals for this particular day were ladies pants for a quarter, ladies skirts for a dime, men's suits and blazers for a buck. Yes, you heard me correctly! I purchased two skirts, one that was from GAP and the other from a major retailer that still had tags on it. I was thrilled beyond belief at the great deals that I scored. With a little time and imagination and shopping savvy, I was able to purchase some items that will coordinate perfectly with other items in my wardrobe and save some cash in the process! What I am trying to say: Don't sleep on the thrift and consignment stores! If thrifting isn't your thing, then hollah at me, I love a good shopping challenge!

unicorns are magical!

Several years ago, my daughter came home and shared a story of a classmate with me. He was sitting at his desk with his hand on his forehead pointing toward the sky. My daughter asked him what he was doing? He replied, "My mother told me that I could be anything that I wanted to be so today, I am a unicorn." With a sigh he said, "and tomorrow I may be a desk" as he placed his hands palms down and his feet squared to the floor. I chuckle each time I think about that story as we all need to be encouraged to be whatever we want to be in this life, including a unicorn or desk if you choose!

U-v

Visualize your legacy

I referenced this earlier in the book, but it is worth saying again. What will you be remembered for? Everyone has the ability to create a legacy in their lifetime. What contributions will you make to others for the betterment of your community? It's easy for people to say nice things about you when you are in their presence. However, what is more important is the impression that you made, and what they say after you have left the room. What will they say about you? Did you make a positive impact? Are you leaving your surroundings a better place than before you came?

I'm reminded of the line from one of my favorite poems by Ralph Waldo Emerson, "To leave the world a bit better, whether by a healthy child, a garden patch or a redeemed social condition: to know that one life has breathed easier because you have lived. This is to have succeeded."

My children and some friends were playing a game called "Would you rather" one night. One of the questions was, would you rather people show up to your wedding or for your funeral? That was an interesting question and the teen's answers were quite interesting as well, but it was definitely a point to ponder.

While we are on **V**, we are a very visual society. We trust that seeing is believing. We not only communicate verbally but non-verbally. Nonverbal communication includes facial expressions, eye contact, tone of voice, body posture and motions. It may also include the clothes we wear. According to an online article on body language ninety-three percent of a first impressions come from non-verbal communication. Seven percent is what you say, thirty-eight percent is the tone of voice, and fifty-five percent is body language. The single most important factor in non-verbal communication is how you feel about yourself, because it shows.

There are specialists who decode body language. Body language is also a part of people's perception of you. The best way to see how you look and hear how you sound is to have someone videotape you. The next time you have to make a class presentation or give a speech have someone videotape you and then review it to see what your body language says about you. Make adjustments accordingly!

While we are on the subject of communication, there is no secret that I love to talk! My grandfather said that I talked more than any child he had ever met! I enjoy talking with other people, hearing their stories and seeing that we have many things in common. I often say that God gave us two ears and one mouth so we should listen twice as much as we talk. However, I have noticed that many people have lost the art of simply talking to each other. In today's technology-driven society, taking the time to talk with someone can still be the most beneficial kind of communication. Try it sometime, put down the telephone, and the iPod, the iPad and limit the text messages and emails. Better yet, try picking up a pen and writing a note.

I love nothing more than going to my mail box and wedged in between the bills and junk mail is a handwritten note. My mom is the best at doing so. Even though she lives an hour away, she will mail me a note, take the time to address the envelope and buy a stamp and put it in the mail. I have picked up this trait from her. Writing a thank you note or adding a personal message on the bottom of a greeting card is perhaps the easiest way to make someone's day and show your appreciation at the same time.

volume-It's not about the volume; it's about the **value** of making it all work together.

While I believe that you should have multiple items like black and white T-shirts, black pumps, boots and jeans that are worn in regular rotation, there are times when volume should not compete with quality items that you can wear over and over, season after season. Versatility is key to making separates work together. This is where being creative can come in handy. I like the features in many fashion magazines where they mix and match 12 key pieces of clothing and turn them into a month's worth of outfits. So BEFORE you go out shopping, take a detailed inventory of what you already have in your closet that could create the perfect outfit!

"It's better to have fewer things of quality than
too much expendable junk." -- Rachel Zoe,
famous fashion stylist to the celebrities.

Mirror, Mirror -- If someone were to decode your body language, what would it say about you? Answer the "Would you rather" question; would you rather have more people show up at your wedding or at your funeral, and why?

W-w

Work what you (already) GOT!

We have all been equipped with the gifts and talents that we need to be successful. It's up to us to take those gifts and talents and make them work positively for us. We are all works in progress. But you've got to put the time in to reap the rewards. Anything worth having is worth working for. That also goes for our body image. Perhaps you want to lose weight, so you say, I'm not going to (you fill in the blank)_____ until I accomplish what personal goal. Well, weight loss, as with other goals is a process. It does NOT happen overnight. Don't be hard on yourself, but enjoy the journey and celebrate the small accomplishments along the way. And while you are in the process of working on your goals, work what you GOT!

wash and wear items mean easy care and savings on your (dry) cleaning bill

Part of what to consider when purchasing an item is how to care for it. Can it be washed or does it need to be dry cleaned? Does it have extra buttons for replacements or extra thread or embellishments? Should it be folded or hung? All these things will help extend the life of the garment and keep it looking as good as new. SIDE NOTE: Sometimes there will be thread stitched in the slits of jackets and skirts. Before wearing these items, gently snip them with scissors and remove the thread. These threads are in place to hold the slit together after the garment is made. This is another place your full length mirror will come in handy for checking out your outfit from the back and making sure that you look awesome coming and going!

Walmart...the things I see there make me shake my head. (SMH)

On a recent trip down the Walmart aisles, I saw a young lady in her mid-twenties with three young boys. She had a nice haircut, but the front of it was hot pink. She had a nice shape, but she had on a pair of leggings that were toooooo thin. So thin, I could see her underwear, and they just so happened to match her hair. I wondered if she consciously left home knowing that the whole world and I - including the young man who was working the register- noticed. She might have thought, "I am JUST going to Walmart to pick up a few things; I won't see anyone that I know" or "I am matching from head to toe and I want to make sure that I get noticed."

Whatever the reason, wearing leggings as pants is a trend that I will be all too glad to see play out. Just as in my day, when *"Da' Butt"* by EU, an R&B group, was atop the charts and the song's accompanying attire was spandex biking shorts. Boy oh Boy... smh! I took part in the biking shorts trend. I was a freshman in college; we would have parties and the dress code was wear as much spandex as you wanted. Back then, there were some folk who did NOT need to help that trend flourish. I didn't think that fashion faux paux would EVER run its course. Biking shorts were designed to wear as exercise gear, in the gym or on the track. Any other way it was worn was really pushing fashion limits. Similarly, the leggings trend can't run its course fast enough (for me!)

All leggings were NOT created equal. They once were a trendy item worn in casual settings, with a shirt long enough to cover the back side. Not so much today, leggings are EVERYWHERE. Some, however, were not made to wear solo. They are too thin, more like hosiery or tights and leave little to the imagination. Jeggings, a cross between leggings and jeans, became popular in the late

2000's, but their popularity peaked in 2010 and became one of the most popular items to have in your closet. Jeggings are made to look more like jeans or pants and give much more coverage than leggings. Fair warning: Check the quality of the leggings before you buy them, a good rule to note is if you can see through them and they were 2 for $ 5, they were more than likely NOT meant to be worn as pants.

While I am on my pet peeves, unless you are going to an organized pajama party, pajama bottoms/sleep/lounge pants and satin sleep bonnets should **NOT** be worn out of the house. There is a reason for this; who wants to interact with someone who literally could have rolled out of the bed and headed out into the real world instantly ready, without perhaps adding water. Take pride in your appearance! You never know who you may run into while making a quick pick up at Walmart.

X-x

Xerox copying someone else is robbing the world of who you were put on this earth to be. No double-sided copies; originals ONLY please!

I was recently watching a show that featured people who were having identity crises. One show featured a woman who has been told that she looked like the actress and model Pamela Anderson Lee. So she started imitating the way Pamela dressed, wore her hair, and enhanced her body to be shaped like the actress. It's been said that flattery is a sincere form of a compliment; however, when does wanting to be so much like another person make you miss out on who YOU are? There is no real harm in admiring another person for their hair or their style of dress, however to lose your own identity in the process is not cool. Stay true to yourself and love being you -- remember everyone else is taken!

(e)xamine yourself and make adjustments accordingly

Try this: Take a look in the mirror and ask yourself, "Would I love ME? Hire ME or date ME? If the person staring back at you says, "No," then make some changes for the better. Take a class, get a mentor, and shadow someone that you admire. Examine, make changes and repeat.

"Trust yourself, Think for yourself, Act for yourself, Speak for yourself, Be yourself; Imitation is suicide"- Marva Collins, American educator, civil rights activist.

Mirror, Mirror -- Do you have an idol or person that you admire? What do you most admire about them and how far would you go to be like another person? How much is too much to change to be like another person?

Y-y

Yesterday's history, tomorrow's a mystery, today's a gift; that's why we call it the present

Carpe Diem is a Latin phrase translated "seize the day"; live it to its fullest, make it count, do the darn thang! Each of us has the same 24 hours in a day. How we spend that time is up to us. What kind of day will you make it? You can spend time complaining about what you don't have or what you want to change, hating on someone else for what they have, or you can take life by the shopping bag handles and make it a BOTO, buy one, get two-free kinda day.

youth... Forever 21 is a store, not a season that lasts forever and ever

There is truth in the saying that age is nothing but a number. BUT...everything has an expiration date, according to an article from greatschools.com. Tween and Teen shoppers make up a large percentage of the market share of money flowing into our malls. They also establish and affect fashion, lifestyle, and overall trends. So you will notice lots of stores that cater to the tween and teen market. Stores that cater to this market are savvy and know what it takes to capture the attention of this vulnerable but valuable consumer. Stores such as Forever 21, H&M, and Charlotte Russe just to name a few are great places to find the season's hottest trends for a great price. However, use caution when creating a complete wardrobe from these stores alone. Remember all bodies are NOT created equal, so what may look fabulous on one body, may not do "justice" to another. As you mature, you will learn more about yourself, what you like and don't like, what looks great on you and what your personal style is. Through this process, your shopping habits and places you shop *should* change as well.

3-3

Zeal, Zest & Zing for life is the key to enjoying a balanced life

Find a passion or a cause that you believe in, never settle for mediocrity, strive for the best in all you do, and be the best YOU that you can be. Life shouldn't be all work and no play but it can't be all play, and no work; there must be a balance. It has been said that if you find your passion or calling in life that you will do it and it won't feel like work.

We all have God-given gifts and talents. It could be singing, poetry, dance or a special skill, like making things with your hands or an eye for photography. Whatever gift(s) you discover you have--use it, share it, and make the world a better place because you possess YOUR gift. Perhaps you aren't sure what your talent is. Ask yourself what you do that comes naturally? What do you enjoy doing for fun? There are also tests such as the Myers Briggs that help you discover your best personality traits and books like "What Color is Your Parachute?" that can assist you with figuring out what career strengths you possess. The key is to discover those strengths and use them to shine!

Mirror, Mirror -- Have you discovered your special talent(s)? If so what is it and how are you using it?

zebra, leopard, cheetah, tiger and giraffe...Oh my!!

You can wear all the animals in the zoo — just not all at the same time. Animal print can be a tricky thing. However worn carefully and in small, targeted doses it can mean the difference between acing the trend or an epic fail. Mixing colors and patterns is something that fashion magazines feature all the time, but there is certainly a difference between runway and real way. As I said earlier in the book, most trends that we see in fashion today we have experienced before and most likely will experience again. Since the animal print trend comes and goes every few years, I would safely say that investing in a piece or two may be a good idea. For example a belt, or shoes, or a scarf, so that when the animal print trend decides to visit again, you'll be ready! As they say, what's old is new again!

Epilogue

I hope that you have enjoyed the book and found some of the tips helpful and perhaps learned something new. Please share with your friends. Remember to respect yourself and others, always look your best and be appropriately dressed for the occasion. Definitely remember fashion should be fun NEVER frustrating! I would love to hear from you. Please contact me at imagematters101@gmail. com!

Fierce, Fabulous & Fashionably Yours,

Glynis

"Beauty is being the best possible version of yourself on the inside and out."-- Author unknown

When I began this journey to write this book, I realized that when I was growing up I had a village of people to help me not only dress and act appropriately, but how to be a lady. Long gone are the days when mom and grandma were the two most influential figures in a young girl's life. Today many of our young ladies may not be fortunate enough to have a village to help them. To the mentors, teachers, big sisters and leaders of our young ladies, WE must become that village. I truly believe that each one of us MUST reach one so that together we become stronger, and equip and encourage our young ladies to be the very best they can be, with the tools and confidence they need to succeed.

Today TV, advertising, the news, social media, YouTube and popular apps are inappropriately shaping, molding, and dressing our girls. This book is designed to inspire and share some simple ways to help young girls be their best whether it's in school, a worship event, internship, hanging out with friends or a date.

Each one must reach one to create a village!

Printed in the United States
By Bookmasters